SIMPLE MACHINES

WHEELS AND AXLES

Nancy Dickmann

BROWN BEAR BOOKS

Published by Brown Bear Books Ltd

4877 N. Circulo Bujia
Tucson, AZ 85718
USA

and

Leroy House
436 Essex Rd
London N1 3QP
UK

© 2018 Brown Bear Books Ltd

ISBN 978-1-78121-403-9 (library bound)
ISBN 978-1-78121-433-6 (paperback)

Library of Congress Cataloging-in-Publication Data available on request

Text: Nancy Dickmann
Design Manager: Keith Davis
Picture Manger: Sophie Mortimer
Editorial Director: Lindsey Lowe
Children's Publisher: Anne O'Daly

Manufactured in the United States of America

CPSIA compliance information: Batch#AG/5608

Picture Credits

The photographs in this book are used by permission and through the courtesy of:

Front Cover: Dreamstime: Ingrid Prats inset; Thinkstock: istock main.
Interior: Dreamstime: Gina Sanders 20l; istockphoto: 6–7, 8–9, 12–13, 14–15, 21t, Lovric drazen 16, Major 16–17, Simon 6; Shutterstock: Krisana Antharith 10–11t, Atiwat Photography 16, Jorg Hackermann 4–5, Dmitry Kalinovsky 2021, Nature Sports 21b, Jo Pepe 11b, Dmitry Sheremeta 12, Tachefoto 4; Thinkstock: istockphoto 18–19.

All other artwork and photography © Brown Bear Books.

t-top, r-right, l-left, c-center, b-bottom

Brown Bear Books has made every attempt to contact the copyright holder. If you have any information please contact:
licensing@brownbearbooks.co.uk

Websites

The website addresses in this book were valid at the time of going to press. However, it is possible that contents or addresses may change following publication of this book. No responsibility for any such changes can be accepted by the author or the publisher. Readers should be supervised when they access the Internet.

Words in **bold** appear in the Useful Words on page 23.

Contents

What Are Wheels and Axles?

Wheels are everywhere. There are wheels on cars and trains. There are wheels in fans and rolling pins. A wheel is a circular object. There is an **axle** at the center. The wheel spins freely around the axle.

WOW!

A car drives on four wheels. The steering wheel helps make the wheels turn.

Wheels and axles make it easier to move heavy objects. They carry weight as they roll along. Wheels can help us move faster.

What Are Machines?

Machines help us do work. They make the force we use more powerful. Wheels are a type of **machine**. A machine with wheels can move heavy objects.

A wheelchair is a machine. It has wheels and axles. Some wheelchairs also have motors.

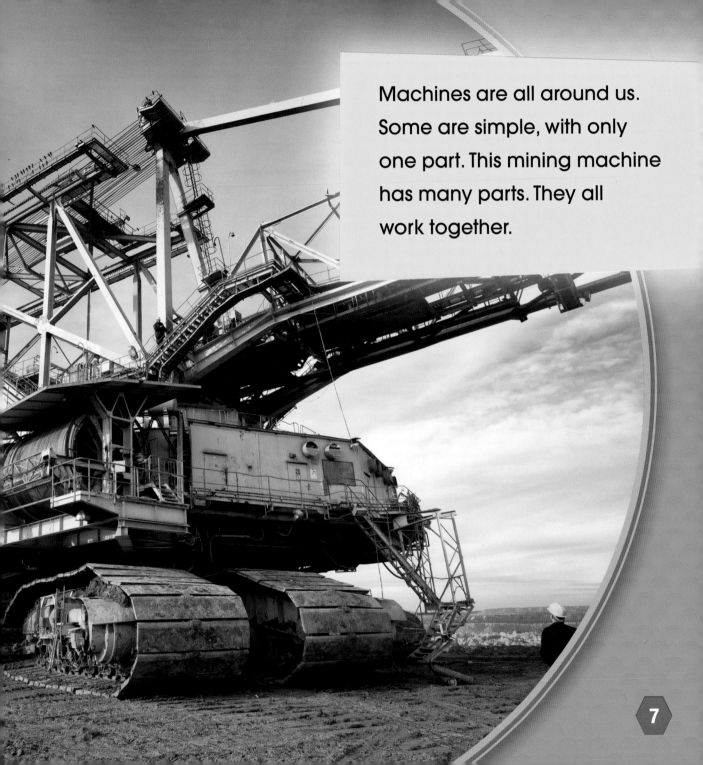

Machines are all around us. Some are simple, with only one part. This mining machine has many parts. They all work together.

Wheels on the Move

When one object slides past another, it makes **friction**. Friction slows down moving objects. Pushing a heavy box across the ground is hard. There is a lot of friction.

Friction

How wheels reduce friction

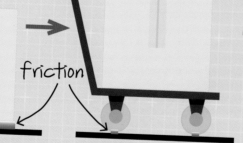

friction

The box is on the ground. There is a lot of friction.

On wheels, there is less friction.

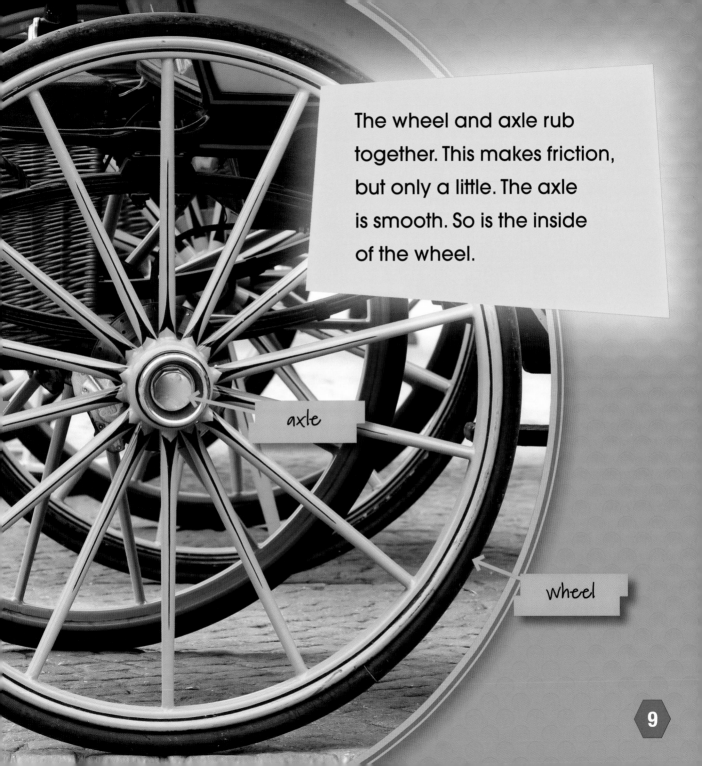

The wheel and axle rub together. This makes friction, but only a little. The axle is smooth. So is the inside of the wheel.

axle

wheel

Wheels and Forces

A **force** is a push or a pull. It takes force to turn a wheel. If we push on the outside, the center turns too. The force is greater at the center.

Turning a wheel

The outside moves a greater distance.

The center doesn't move as far. That makes the force stronger.

A doorknob is a wheel. We turn its outer edge. This makes the spindle at the center turn. It opens the latch.

WOW!

Some wheels can be sharp. A pizza cutter has a wheel. Its sharp edges slice the pizza.

Wheels in the Past

Before wheels were invented, people used rollers. Many rollers were just logs. They did not have axles. They were put under heavy objects. Then the object could be pushed along.

WOW!

The first wheels were not for vehicles. People used them to make pots.

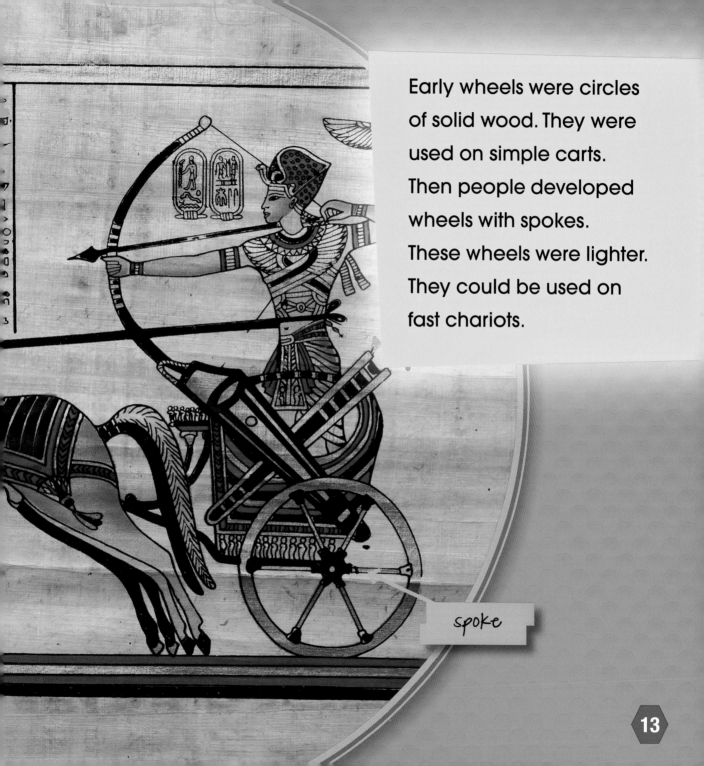

Early wheels were circles of solid wood. They were used on simple carts. Then people developed wheels with spokes. These wheels were lighter. They could be used on fast chariots.

spoke

Wheels Today

We use wheels all the time. There are small wheels on roller skates. Trucks have big wheels. A bulldozer has wheels inside its tracks. Some wheels can be fun. We ride on Ferris wheels.

WOW!

Some trucks have huge wheels. They spread out a heavy weight. They won't sink into the ground.

A wind turbine is a type of wheel. Wind makes the blades spin. This makes the **axle** in the center turn around. Its motion is turned into electricity.

Everyday Wheels

There are wheels in your home. A bicycle has wheels. So do toy cars and trains. Even some furniture has wheels. The wheels make it easier to move around.

WOW!

Animals can use wheels, too! Hamsters have wheels for exercise. When they run, it turns the wheel.

A fan is a kind of wheel. The motor makes the **axle** turn. This turns the blades. They blow out cooling air.

Compound Machines

Wheels and axles are simple machines.
A **lever** is a simple **machine**, too.
Simple machines can work together.
They form a **compound machine**.

A wheelbarrow's handles are levers. They make it easier to lift a heavy **load**. The wheel lets you push the load more easily.

wheel

lever

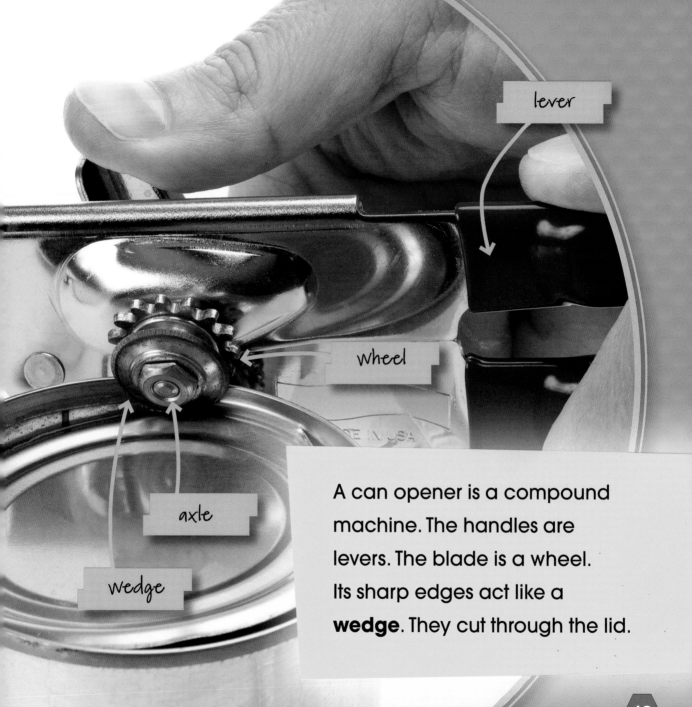

lever

wheel

axle

wedge

A can opener is a compound machine. The handles are levers. The blade is a wheel. Its sharp edges act like a **wedge**. They cut through the lid.

Spot the Wheel!

Can you find the wheels in these pictures?

1

2

3

5

4

Try It!

Rollers are a simple type of wheel, with no axle. Can they make it easier to move something?

You will need:

- a heavy book
- about 10 round pencils or markers (all the same size)
- a friend to help you

1. Put the book on the floor, then try to push it along. How hard is it?

3. Put the book on top of the pencils.

4. Start pushing the book.

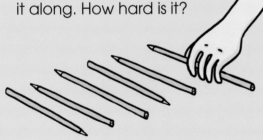

2. Lay the pencils out in a row. These are your rollers.

5. Whenever a pencil gets left behind, your friend should pick it up and move it to the front.

Is it easier to push the book on the floor or on the rollers?

Useful Words

axle The shaft that goes through the center of a wheel.

compound machine A machine that is made up of smaller machines. It can have several different simple machines.

force A push or a pull.

friction The rubbing of one object against another.

lever Type of simple machine. A lever has a long beam that rests on a point called a pivot.

load The object that a machine tries to move.

machine Something that helps us do work. Machines use energy to do a job.

wedge A simple machine with angled sides. Wedges can split things apart.

Answers to page 20–21: Did you spot the wheels?
1. The wheelchair's wheels; **2.** the steering wheel;
3. the dump truck's wheels; **4.** the race cars'
wheels; **5.** the ceiling fan.

Find out More

Websites
www.britannica.com/
technology/simple-machine

www.explainthatstuff.com/
howwheelswork.html

www.idahoptv.org/sciencetrek/
topics/simple_machines/facts.
cfm

Books
Hauling a Pumpkin: Wheels and Axles vs. Lever Mari Schuh, Lerner Classroom 2015

Wheels and Axles
Sian Smith, Heinemann 2012

Wheels and Axles in Action
Gillian Gosman, PowerKids Press, 2010

Index